CONNECTING
READING AND WRITING
in the Intermediate Grades

A Workshop Approach

Diane M. Cohle
Hatboro-Horsham
School District
Horsham, Pennsylvania,
USA

Wendy Towle
Tredyffrin-Easttown
School District
Berwyn, Pennsylvania,
USA

INTERNATIONAL
Reading
Association

800 Barksdale Road, PO Box 8139
Newark, Delaware 19714-8139, USA
www.reading.org

Library of Congress Cataloging in Publication Data
Cohle, Diane M.
    Connecting reading and writing in the intermediate grades: a workshop/
Diane M. Cohle, Wendy Towle.
        p.   cm.
Includes bibliographical references (p.   ).
    ISBN 0-87207-296-7 (alk. paper)
        1. Language arts (Elementary)   2. Group work in education.   I. Towle, Wendy.
II. Title.
LB1576.T685   2001   2001000414
372.6–dc21

Contents

Introduction

As with many great inventions, the idea for this book developed out of necessity. In 1987, we began our educational collaboration while teaching in the primary grades—one of us as a regular classroom teacher and the other as a special education teacher. During that time, our school district initiated a program that focused on developmentally appropriate practices in grades K through 2, at the heart of which was the fundamental idea that we as teachers should take each child from where he is and move him forward, while incorporating into our classrooms teaching strategies that work for every child in the classroom. Manipulatives-based math, project-centered learning, and a literacy-centered philosophy were all components of this initiative.

This was not the first time we had been introduced to the literacy-centered philosophy, and we embraced the new curriculum wholeheartedly. Our primary-grade program incorporated many activities involving various aspects of writing, reading, speaking, and listening. We were involved in numerous staff development workshops, and collaboration among teachers was widespread. Parent communication was high, so the transition from a "traditional" program to a new developmentally appropriate philosophy was a smooth one for parents as well.

Several years ago, we both moved from the primary grades to positions in which we were able to gauge the development of our students once they moved beyond Grade 2. Wendy moved on to a fifth-grade teaching position, and Diane assumed the role of Reading Specialist for the school and, several years later, Language Arts Coordinator for the school district. After only a few months in our new positions, we quickly began to understand much more of the "big picture" of language arts instruction within our building and district.

Our district now had a firmly established, developmentally appropriate primary-grade program in place. This program philosophy was one that we strongly felt could and should be extended through the intermediate grades. However, when we revisited much of the information we had received as primary-grade teachers, it was clear that literacy-centered and developmentally appropriate practices were not topics that had been given much attention in grades 3, 4, and 5. We did not have all the pieces to continue what we had started.

Our solution to this dilemma was one that most good teachers have used at one point or another—adaptation. We looked at the components that we found most valuable in the primary grades, and we assessed which ones could be adapted and developed into a plan that would provide an appropriate language arts experience for students in the intermediate grades. The results of that analysis were the implementation of a workshop approach for both reading and writing that was easily integrated into existing curricular needs and that addressed many of the components needed for balanced language arts instruction.

What we hope to present in this book is a framework for other intermediate-grade teachers who wish to use a workshop approach in their classrooms. Our ideas and plans are by no means set in stone. We are constantly revising and refining our vision based on the needs of our students and the ever-evolving research conducted by experts such as Lucy Calkins and Donald Graves. We have worked hard to develop a plan that captures the best practices we knew as primary-grade teachers and extends the literacy-centered philosophy to a whole new group of educators.

In Chapter 1 of this book, we discuss the many benefits of the workshop approach to reading and writing and provide research that supports the implementation of the workshop model. Chapter 2 outlines the various components that may be included in a reading-writing workshop and encourages readers to evaluate their specific needs in order to develop an appropriate workshop for their students. Formal and informal assessment and evaluation are addressed in Chapter 3. Chapter 4 can be considered the "putting it all together" chapter, and it includes ideas for classroom set-up and a discussion of how to frame expectations for the workshop with students. In the last chapter, actual focus lessons and discussion questions are included. Finally, the Appendix provides samples of assessment and record-keeping forms.

As you read this book, we hope that you will recognize the workshop approach for the valuable tool it is—a framework for providing instruction to meet the needs of all learners and to develop a lifelong love of reading and writing in students.

Why Use the Workshop Approach?

ntuitively, using a workshop approach seems "right" to many teachers. But when attempting to implement a philosophical change, such as a shift to a more literacy-centered language arts program, it is imperative that there be support from research for such a change. Parents, teachers, and administrators want to know how a change will benefit students. In this chapter, we build a case for the literacy-centered, workshop approach using research and opinions from experts in a variety of fields, thereby establishing the foundation of our workshop program.

The Teaching-Learning Cycle

During the 1990s, a great deal of language arts research has come out of Australia and New Zealand (Education Department of Western Australia, 1994; Eggleton & Windsor, 1995; New Zealand Ministry of Education, 1997). Literacy-centered learning has strong support in New Zealand schools, and U.S. teachers have adopted many strategies and beliefs developed from the New Zealand model.

One of the most valuable tools to come out of New Zealand is the teaching-learning cycle (see Figure 1, page 6). As we developed a plan for our workshop program, we constantly went back to the teaching-learning cycle and eventually recognized it to be the foundation of all good literacy-centered classrooms.

In the teaching-learning cycle, the notion of traditional assessment, evaluation, and teaching is somewhat reversed: Assessment and evalua-

FIGURE 1
THE TEACHING-LEARNING CYCLE

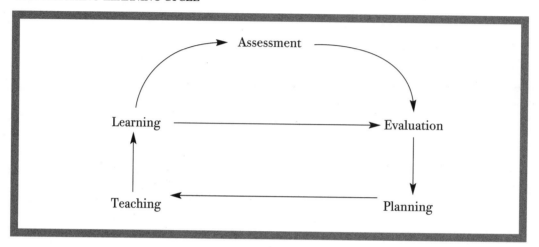

tion become the tools for planning and teaching—not merely the test to measure how much students have learned. Planning leads to teaching, which leads to learning, and the cycle begins again as assessment and evaluation occur and lead to effective future planning. The workshop approach naturally supports this cycle by providing opportunities for frequent assessment and evaluation and by using reading and writing as tools for learning. Additionally, students are asked to assess and evaluate their own learning and to set goals for future learning.

Support From Research

LEARNING-PROCESS RESEARCH

Researchers and educators have long believed that much remains to be learned about the human brain and what is needed to nourish its growth and development. Recently, several prominent experts in the field of brain-based research have published their findings. According to Susan Kovalik (1995), brain-based research indicates that the brain operates best when the following conditions are present:

1. There is an absence of fear.

2. Information is presented and connected in a meaningful way.

3. Sufficient time is provided to process information.

4. Immediate feedback is received.

5. Opportunities exist for collaboration.

6. Opportunities exist for choice.

7. Stimulation occurs through an enriched environment.

In accordance with Kovalik's model, workshop teachers provide meaningful, timely feedback to students in a literacy-rich environment; students work collaboratively with peers and the teacher; and students have choices in their reading, writing, and responding.

In his research in the area of multiple intelligences, Howard Gardner (1993, p. 7) explains, "In my view, the purpose of school should be to develop intelligences and to help people reach vocational and avocational goals that are appropriate to their particular spectrum of intelligences." If we are to encourage and stimulate the development of each child's various intelligences, frequent assessment is imperative. Again, the use of a workshop approach helps teachers not only to frequently assess students, but also to assess them in a variety of ways. Students also are encouraged to experiment with responses that stimulate and utilize a variety of intelligences. This opportunity for varied responses helps students to discover and cultivate their strengths and opens doors to a new awareness of what it means to be "intelligent."

LITERACY RESEARCH

According to the National Reading Panel's (2000) study of best practices in the teaching of reading, children best acquire and strengthen reading skills in an environment that provides varied and meaningful literacy experiences in authentic settings. One framework for providing such a learning environment is the Four Blocks approach to literacy (Cunningham

& Hall, 1999), which was developed for teachers who believe that children need numerous opportunities to read and write, and that children learn to read and write in different ways. In this model, students participate in four distinct strands of literacy learning: guided reading, self-selected reading, working with words, and writing block. Teachers provide direct instruction to small groups of students during the guided reading block. Phonics and spelling instruction occur during the working-with-words block. Cunningham and Hall suggest that a workshop approach is the most effective way to address the blocks of self-selected reading and writing. Not only is the workshop time effective, but teachers have the opportunity to meet regularly with individual children and to frequently assess and evaluate learning.

Classroom Community

In *Variability Not Disability*, Cathy Roller (1996) writes, "Rather than view children as capable or disabled, workshop classrooms assume that children are different, that each child is unique and has unique interests and abilities, and that differences are normal" (p. 7). Perhaps one of the strongest arguments for implementing a workshop program is the ease with which teachers can accommodate the needs of all students within this setting. Students at all levels of ability and with all areas of interests are able to read and write in ways that are meaningful to them. In this way, a feeling of success for all is incorporated into a community where all students are viewed as capable of learning.

Lucy Calkins (1991) further discusses the idea of a supportive classroom community in *Living Between the Lines*. As teachers, our role is to help students move from their current level to the next level of learning. One way to engender the love of learning among students is to find ways to make learning personally significant to each child. Calkins writes, "Teachers of writing and reading throughout the world have come to care passionately about workshop teaching, in part because reading and writing are ways in which human beings find significance and direction, beauty and intimacy, in their lives." Calkins continues by describing the importance of shared experiences and stories in the building of a supportive learning community. The workshop program provides for shared experiences to occur in a natural and ongoing way. Children are encouraged to share their experiences as readers and writers. These experiences accumulate and build on one another, and the class creates a shared history of literacy together.

National Standards and Shifts in Classrooms

The push toward more rigorous academic standards for U.S. students has left many teachers wondering how such high expectations are ever to be met—especially for those students who are struggling with the current curriculum. The International Reading Association (IRA)/National Council of Teachers of English (NCTE) publication, *Standards for the English Language Arts* (1996), suggests that students should "apply a wide range of strategies to comprehend, interpret, evaluate, and appreciate texts," and "participate as knowledgeable, reflective, creative, and critical members of a variety of literacy communities" (p. 25). These are the same types of learning that the workshop classroom fosters. Workshop classrooms not only follow the design set forth by the *Standards for the English Language Arts*. They also provide an environment where all students are able to succeed and to develop a foundation that will enable them to become proficient in those areas.

In *Educating Everybody's Children* (Cole, 1995), the contributors recognize that the idea of a set of national standards, which assumes that all students will achieve minimum competency in the skills and content designated for each subject area, is one that requires a paradigm shift for many teachers. Teachers must increase their repertoire of strategies and rethink the fundamental set-up of their classrooms to discover ways in which they can help all students to move ahead and grow as learners.

Eileen and Wheaton Griffin (1994) address this paradigm shift through their research, which focuses on developmentally appropriate practices and the value of creating a student-centered classroom. When attempting to move from a more traditional educational setting to one that is developmentally appropriate, the Griffins suggest a number of shifts that must take place. Educational philosophy must change—from children adapting to schools adapting—from child as dependent to child as a partner in knowledge construction—from assessment for classification and reporting to assessment for making instructional decisions—from paper and pencil representations of knowledge to multiple ways of representing knowledge.

What the Griffins describe in their analysis of this paradigm shift is what occurs in a workshop classroom: Students read and write to make connections, and students use reading and writing as tools for learning. Using assessment as a tool for planning allows teachers the opportunity to build a classroom program that provides for the needs and interests of all their students. Finally, in a workshop classroom, the students are active learners who collaborate with the teacher in constructing their own knowledge, thus making their learning more meaningful.

In summing up the benefits of the workshop classroom, we point to the support from research in both literacy and learning. We also find support in the national standards and in the components of the theory of developmentally appropriate practices. Last, we rely on our experiences in the classroom, which clearly show that the workshop approach provides the freedom and the strategies necessary to meet the individual needs of all students.

Setting Up the Workshop

A reading-writing workshop can be implemented in a variety of forms. It can be integrated into an existing language arts program or, just as easily, it can become the core of a newly designed program. We have seen the workshop framework presented to an entire elementary school faculty, and when the workshop was used in the classroom, no two teachers implemented it in exactly the same way.

The reading and writing components of the workshop should flow seamlessly into one another. Quite often, when observing students in action, it may be difficult to distinguish which component of the workshop is actually in process. However, for the ease of explanation, we have separated each component and delineated the essential elements. Although these descriptions provide the framework for establishing a workshop approach, they are not the only methods of implementation. Certainly, as you begin using the workshop components in the classroom, you will make adaptations in order to more fully meet the needs of your individual students.

The Writing Component

Student writing is the heart of the writing component of the workshop. Students write every day for a variety of meaningful purposes. Teachers aid students in discovering what makes "good writing." Students develop the ability to reflect on and evaluate their own writing. Students and teachers work together to share ideas and refine and revise writing.

Students learn that writing is a process through which they can communicate effectively with the world around them.

WRITER'S NOTEBOOKS

In *The Art of Teaching Writing*, Lucy Calkins (1994) describes in great detail the use of writer's notebooks in a response-centered classroom. Children keep these notebooks with them at all times. They are encouraged to start looking at the world around them through the eyes of a writer. Ordinary things become extraordinary. Students write in their notebooks whenever they see, hear, or read something they think is significant. After several weeks of writing, students are given time to reflect on the entries in their notebooks. The goal is to look for any themes that might be developing in the writing. For instance, perhaps a student has a number of entries about a variety of topics, but in each entry there is mention of his brother. It becomes obvious that the brother is an important figure in the student's life and, with guidance from the teacher, the student may use the information in the notebook to write about the significance of his brother in his life.

The goal of the writer's notebook is not always a finished story. Calkins believes we write to learn more about ourselves. If the student's reflections lead her to write a letter to a friend outlining some unresolved feelings or conflicts, that is perfectly appropriate. Some days, students may find themselves copying a passage from a book they are reading into their own notebook because they really enjoy the particular language the author has used and wish to model similar language in future writings.

Writing takes many forms and occurs for many reasons. Through the use of writer's notebooks, children can begin to see the vast uses of the written word—both for communication and creative expression. One sixth-grade student used her notebook as a place to try different approaches to a specific topic, and she has begun the process of self-revising and editing, coming up with a unique style for accomplishing this task (see Figure 2).

FIGURE 2
NOTEBOOK ENTRY

> The evergreen tree stands lone and majestic in the field
> of grass, In deep contrast with the dreamy azure of the sky. /summer
> Standing tall, reigning over all that ~~take refuge~~ live below it, it is
> still humble. Its branches raise up towards ~~the~~ a sun ~~a~~
>
> As the / that is no longer there
> sun sinks / ~~golden bauble~~, as if ~~it is~~ worshipping some power unknown.
> below the / ~~As the sun's last rays~~ its last rays glide over the ~~horizons~~ field: the tree
> horizon, / is lit up with a brilliant glow. It suddenly grows dim as the
> sun says a final goodbye. I start to run to the tree,

WRITING CONFERENCES

Each day while students write in their writer's notebooks or work on publishing completed works, the teacher conducts individual student conferences. These conferences are the place where teacher and student really connect—and where direct, individualized instruction can occur. It is important that each conference has a goal, although that goal may be different for each student on any given day. Conferences may be used for information gathering; for sharing ideas; or for direct instruction on mechanics, style, or form. After a conference, students should have a goal for the next step in their writing process. Anecdotal notes, recorded and kept by the teacher, are a valuable tool for holding productive conferences, setting goals, and providing important information for assessment and evaluation (see Appendix, Forms 13 and 14).

During conferences, many teachers may feel unsure about how to approach a student and his writing. Certainly, the purpose of the conference should not be for the teacher to rewrite the student's work in a more mechanically acceptable form, but should be approached as a way for the teacher to connect with each student writer. Graves (1991) provides a list of sample questions to generate discussion during a conference:

- Can you tell me how you happened to choose this topic?

- Can you remember the moment you first thought of this?

- What did you hope would happen because you wrote this?

- What did you hope to learn?

- Did this have any connection with anything you've written before? Is it anything like a topic you've written about before?

- When did you start this piece?

- Did you run into any stumbling blocks? Anything slow you down so far?

- What is this piece about?

- What have you just worked on? What are you working on now?

- How is it going?

- Have you spoken about it with anyone recently?

- How did it go this morning?

- What do you think will happen next?

- How do you think it will end?

- Who will read this?

- What will you do with it when you finish?

- What will you write next?

- How do you think you will write the next part? (p. 98)

PUBLISHING

As stated earlier, not every piece of writing must be taken to the formal publishing stage. However, if children are truly going to view themselves as writers, it is necessary for them to have authentic purposes for publishing and sharing. Publishing can take many forms—a grocery list, a letter, or a personal memoir. A highlight of our school year was a book publishing project (see Figure 3) in which fifth-grade students worked coopera-

FIGURE 3
PICTURE BOOK PROJECT

We are going to study the genre of the picture book. Our assignment will be two-fold: First, we will read and analyze a variety of picture books in order to determine the qualities that are a part of all great picture books. Second, we will work with partners to create our own picture books using an idea from our Writer's Notebooks and our list of picture book qualities. Each partner will receive a copy of the completed book, and copies also will go the library.

Directions

1. With your partner, please choose several different picture books that really appeal to you. After you have read your books, use the attached form to list at least five qualities that you believe are necessary to create a great picture book. We will share these ideas and then develop a class list.

2. After our list of qualities is complete, go back to your Writer's Notebooks and look for an idea that could be used for your picture book story. Remember to keep in mind the qualities we have listed that a great picture book must have.

3. You and your partner now write your story. As you develop the storyline, remember to think about pictures ideas, too.

4. Once your story is complete, schedule a conference with the teacher. After the conference, you may need to revise or edit for mechanical errors.

5. When you complete the rough draft and have revised and edited as necessary, you may type your story on the computer. If you use ClarisWorks, your teacher can help you set up the story so it can be printed in book format using Click Book.

6. After your story has been printed in book format, you and your partner must complete the illustrations. Draw all illustrations in pencil first and then go over them in black pen. Your book then will be sent to the copy center.

7. You will receive four copies of your book. The illustrations in each copy must be colored in neatly, and then you will bind your book using the directions provided by the teacher.

8. Each partner gets one copy of the book, and other copies are donated to the library.

FIGURE 4
PICTURE BOOK SAMPLE

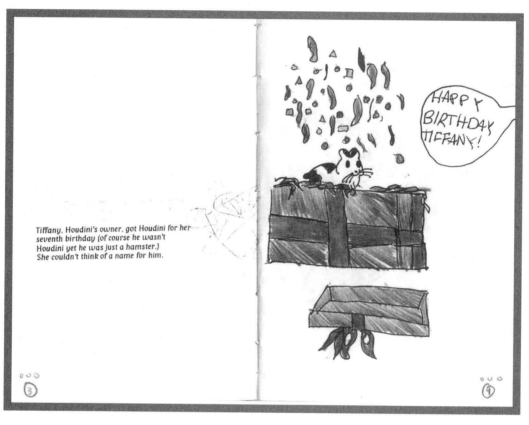

A postcard activity (see Figure 5) completed by a fourth-grade class shows how teachers can tie specific objectives to classroom activities in meaningful ways (see Figure 6). Certainly, all publishing need not be so elaborate. Posting book reviews on a classroom bulletin board is an equally meaningful opportunity. Once again, the needs and interests of your students will help you to determine the best publishing avenues for them.

FIGURE 5
POSTCARD ACTIVITY

Dear Class,

I'm in Sandusky, Ohio looking over lake Erie and Cedar Point. Once we got to Cedar Point, we ran to "Power Tower". You sit in a seat, go up 300ft and lunch down and it does 5 g's! I also rode 13 other coasters! But the best part was when we went on "Mantis". It's a stand-up coaster that goes upsidedown 7 times and it's 175ft high. I had a blast! Wish you were here!

Jeff W

Mrs Roberts' class
100 Maple Ave
Anywhere, USA

Pokemon

	STUDENT	TEACHER
I started my paragraph with a good topic sentence.	✓	✓
I gave 3 or 4 good supporting detail sentences that told more about my topic.	✓	✓
My ending has a good concluding sentence.	✓	✓
My sentences are interesting and complete.	✓	✓
My ideas are clear and give enough information.	✓	✓
I have a good concluding sentence that lists a special highlight.	✓	✓
My picture is colorful, neat and attractive.	✓	✓
My address and stamp are correctly completed.	✓	✓
I capitalized proper nouns and sentence beginnings.	✓	✓
I punctuated sentence endings.	✓	✓
I used commas where necessary.	✓	✓
All words are spelled correctly.	✓	✓
I indented my paragraph.	✓	✓

FIGURE 6
SPECIFIC OBJECTIVES OF POSTCARD ACTIVITY

1. Write with a sharp, distinct focus identifying topic, task, and audience.
2. Write using well-developed content appropriate for the topic.
   - Write paragraphs that have a topic and supporting details.
3. Revise writing to improve organization and word choice; check the logic, order of ideas, and precision of vocabulary.
4. Edit writing using the conventions of language.
   - Spell common, frequently used words correctly.
   - Use capital letters correctly.
   - Punctuate correctly.
   - Use complete sentences.
5. Present and defend written work for publication when appropriate.

The Reading Component

Although similar to Sustained Silent Reading (SSR), the reading component of the workshop differs from traditional SSR in three major aspects. First, children have choices in their reading, but the choices come from books that are written at the student's independent reading level. Second, children meet on a regular basis with the teacher and their peers to discuss what they are reading. Third, in addition to merely reading a book, students have the option of creating a personal response to the books they read. In reading workshop, students learn to read independently for three purposes: reading for literacy experience, reading for information, and reading to perform a task. The conferences and assessment allow the teacher to easily determine if these goals are being met.

INDEPENDENT READING

Given the proper planning and assessment, independent reading time can be the single most important part of the teaching of reading. Because students read and discuss books at their independent reading level during reading workshop, it is here that they develop a lifelong love of reading and a deeper understanding of what it means to be a competent reader. However, if students are left without guidance and support in the selection and discussion of their books, teachers can lose valuable opportunities for instruction.

The first key to a successful independent reading program is a large, varied, and leveled classroom library. The library should be inviting, and reading levels of books should be easily discernible by students. Additionally, the teacher must determine each student's independent reading level in order to point students to appropriate book choices. There are several methods for determining reading levels (see Chapter 3). Students must be taught an easy way to help them determine whether a book is too hard, too easy, or just right for them. One quick method we have used successfully is the "five-finger" method in which students read a page from a book and hold up one finger for each word they do not know. If by the end of the page they have five fingers up, the book is too difficult.

Once students choose their books, depending on the age and competency of students and the goals of the teacher, they might read alone silently or aloud with a partner or small group. Students are responsible for keeping track of what and how much they read each day. If reading is required for homework, remind students to take their reading-workshop book home to read as well. This guarantees that students read appropriately leveled books both in school and at home.

READING CONFERENCES

Reading conferences should be scheduled on a regular basis, and this scheduling can be handled in a number of different ways (see Chapters 3 and 4). Ideally, each student should sign up for one conference every week or two (see Appendix, Form 3). During this time, students may discuss ideas from the book; share plans for a response; request help with editing, proofreading, or fine-tuning a response; request assistance in choosing a new book; or talk about their reading in general. Conferences can be used to make frequent checks on students' progress and comprehension and guide them toward reading both fiction and nonfiction (see Appendix, Forms 4–7).

As with writing conferences, reading conferences are the times when a teacher can directly interact with students about the books they are reading. It is important for a goal to be set at the end of each reading conference and for the student to work toward achieving that goal. The goal should be attainable but should also challenge the student in order for her to make progress as a reader. One useful tool for keeping track of conferences and student goals is a laminated chart with a square for each student. The teacher writes the student's name and goal on a sticky note, and then the student posts the note on the chart in his square. This provides a visual representation of class goals and allows students to look for others who share the same goal.

BOOK RESPONSES

Depending on the grade level and interests of the students, book responses can take many forms, but all are a way for students to make personal connections to what they are reading. The key is for a student to choose the response that she feels is most appropriate for the book she has read and that reflects something important she has learned from reading the story. Additionally, the wide variety of possible responses gives teachers a chance to address the notion of multiple intelligences (Gardner, 1993) in their classrooms. For example, students who have a great deal of artistic ability may create a response that allows them to share their artistic talent, while students who are musically inclined have the freedom to design a response that incorporates a love of music. One fifth-grade learning-support student (with a learning disability) wrote a song after reading a nonfiction book about motorcycles (see Figure 7) and later brought in a guitar and performed it for the class.

FIGURE 7
BOOK RESPONSE—SONG

"Harleys""

A Song

By Jon Ziskowski

Harleys they're real fast.
They started back from the past.
My step-dad, Phil, he's getting one, too.
It's going to be chrome-painted cherry red.
He's going to have a leather seat with leather bags,
too.
It's gonna' go fast,
and it's gonna' have a big, bad engine.
He's gonna like it a lot!

(To be accompanied by guitar)

To illustrate the connection between writing and reading workshop components, one fifth-grade student wrote a letter to a classmate about a book for which the teacher provided clearly defined criteria for the evaluation of the writing (see Figure 8). The student then created a book jacket as her personal reading response (see Figure 9).

Each completed reading response is evaluated by the teacher, using criteria that all students are familiar with from the beginning of the year. Evaluations are discussed with students, who are given an opportunity to reflect on their evaluations in writing. The actual evaluation criteria are based in part on the needs of the students, but they mainly are reflective of the goals the teacher has set for the students within the context of the reading workshop. For example, one goal for our fifth-grade students is

FIGURE 8
WRITING EVALUATION

My Favorite Book
Standard Writing Rubric

Name Michelle Crooks   Date 9/22/99   Michelle

1.4 Types of Writing – Letters	Yes	No
My letter has a heading.	✓	—
My letter has a greeting.	✓	—
My letter has a closing.	✓	—
My letter has a signature.	✓	—

1.4 Types of Writing – Persuasive

I have clearly stated my opinion of a particular book.	✓	—
I have included at least three reasons why the book was enjoyable to me.	✓	—

1.5 Quality of Writing – Mechanics

I have focused on the topic.	✓	—
I have used capital letters correctly- names, beginning of sentences.	✓	—
I have used punctuation correctly.	✓	—
I have spelled words correctly.	✓	—

I have written at least one declarative sentence.
It's called Harry Potter and the Sorcerer's Stone.
I have written at least one imperative sentence.
You have to read this book.
I have written at least one exclamatory sentence.
I loved how the author had some cliffhanger chapters!
I have written at least one interrogative sentence.
How are you?

Title and Author

I have included the title of the story and the author's name in my letter. ✓

Dear Lauren,
    How are you? I just read a really g
book. It's called Harry Potter and the Sorcerer's Sto
I really liked the book because every par
it was exciting. The book is part of a seri
The third book is out and I can't wait to
it! I loved how the author had some
cliffhanger chapters! The second book was
too. I liked the first book because it it
fantasy and I enjoy fantasy books. You
have to read this book

                    Your friend,
                    Michelle

FIGURE 9
BOOK RESPONSE—BOOK JACKET

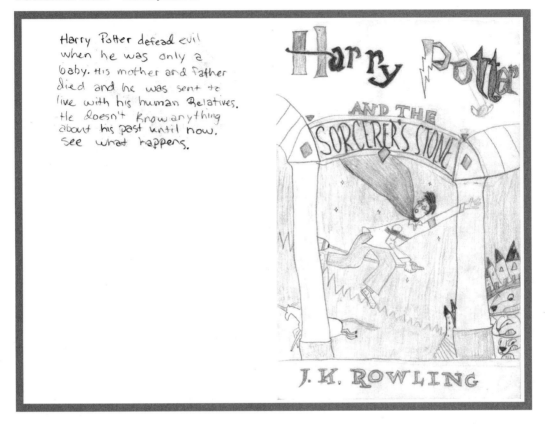

for them to be able to write a concise but informative summary of their books utilizing the five Ws—who, what, where, when, and why. Therefore, summarizing is one of the descriptors on the evaluation sheet that we use in fifth grade.

STUDENT SHARING

The last key component of a reading workshop is the opportunity for student sharing. Students must know that there is a purpose for their reading and responses. Certainly, the enjoyment of reading, the chance to learn something new, and the idea of making personal connections with the book are all fine reasons to participate in the reading workshop program. However, we have found that another prime motivator for many students is the opportunity to share responses and opinions about books with their peers. The sharing sessions need not be very long, nor must they occur every day. But, by allowing students to share their responses on a regular basis, they begin to understand that these responses are valued, not just "busy work" that the teacher assigns. Also, when students hear another student recommend a book, they are much more likely to pick up that book and read it than if the recommendation came from the teacher. It is amazing to hear the amount of independent book discussion that occurs among students in a class that has incorporated the reading workshop program.

Focus Lessons

An extremely important part of the workshop approach to language arts instruction are focus lessons. They are used throughout all areas of the language arts and, most often, are based on the needs of the particular students in the class.

When introducing various strands of the language arts program at the beginning of the year, focus lessons are a valuable tool for establishing procedures and expectations. Teachers model how to work through the various components of the program and clearly delineate expectations and requirements. For many students, the workshop approach is a new experience, so having a solid framework is essential to the success of the program.

Once the program is in progress, focus lessons take place to address questions, strategies, skills, or insights that might arise in students' individual reading or writing. Focus lessons usually occur on an as-needed basis, and they may involve one student, a small group of students, or the whole class. (See Chapter 5 for topics for focus lessons.)

Whole-Group Novels and Anthologies

When scheduled on a daily basis, the reading workshop has the potential to stand alone as the class reading program. However, for a variety of reasons, teachers also may choose to incorporate some type of whole-group reading program into the daily schedule. A number of teachers use a novel or an anthology as the core of the reading program and then supplement this with the reading workshop. The whole-group instruction time is used to explore mechanical or literary skills and vocabulary that are important to all class members. Additionally, some teachers use novels as a tie-in to other curriculum areas (i.e., social studies) and prefer to use whole-group instruction for that purpose.

In keeping with the philosophy associated with developmentally appropriate practices (Griffin, 1994), teachers may differentiate follow-up assignments even when working with a whole-group novel or anthology. Student assignments can be assigned according to interest or skill groups—whichever the teacher feels is necessary for that particular assignment.

Book Discussion Groups

An alternative to traditional whole-group reading instruction, book discussion groups provide the opportunity for students to read and talk about books in a small-group setting. Classroom discussion groups follow the same format as book discussion groups in which many adults are involved. Groups select a book to read over a designated period of time, and the students then alternate between reading and discussion days throughout each week. Each group is responsible for setting the pace of the reading and for designing homework assignments and follow up, such as developing questions for discussions and taking notes in preparation for the next meeting.

Several prerequisite conditions are needed for students to receive the most benefit from book discussion groups. First, because all students in a group read the same book and are expected to work within the same time frame, the group should be composed of students with like abilities. Lucy Calkins (1995) suggests that students write letters to the teacher suggesting classmates whom they feel would be most supportive to them as readers. Most of the time, students have a good sense of their own strengths and weaknesses and choose appropriate peers to work with. However, the teacher ultimately must make a final decision that will benefit all of the students involved.

The second important factor contributing to the success of book groups is experience with book discussion, and both oral and written response. For this reason, we suggest implementing book discussion groups some time in the middle of the school year, after students have had numerous opportunities for open-ended book talks and responses. (See Chapter 4 for information about scheduling book discussion groups.)

Finally, in order to succeed as members of a book discussion group, students must have a sense of responsibility and be able to complete assignments independently. They must be able to work productively in a small-group setting without a great deal of teacher direction or guidance.

Book discussion groups can be implemented as a part of the reading component of the workshop or as a separate component of the language arts program. We have found several sources to be helpful in designing and implementing book discussion groups, including *Book Talk and Beyond* (Martinez & Roser, 1995) and *Lively Discussions!* (Gambrell & Almasi, 1996).

3

Record Keeping and Assessment

Record keeping, assessment, and evaluation provide the basis for planning and teaching in the workshop classroom, and these tasks are the responsibility of both the students and the teacher. Assessment is frequent and ongoing, and it takes a variety of forms.

Student Record Keeping

Students have specific responsibilities for record keeping in both components of the workshop. As part of the reading workshop, students are required to log what and how much they read each day, and some teachers also have students note the different genres they read (see Appendix, Form 1). A similar but simpler form is used for younger students (see Appendix, Form 2). Figure 10 (page 28) illustrates a fifth-grade student's record of books read during reading workshop. Note that entries based solely on in-school reading create gaps in page numbers; therefore, we found it helpful for students to record their out-of-school reading as well.

For younger students and for reluctant readers, we found it helpful to have students complete a reading contract on a regular basis. Sample statements for the contract include:

I will read _____ books/pages per month/week/day.

I will keep a daily reading log.

I will share opinions about what I am reading.

FIGURE 10
SAMPLE READING LOG

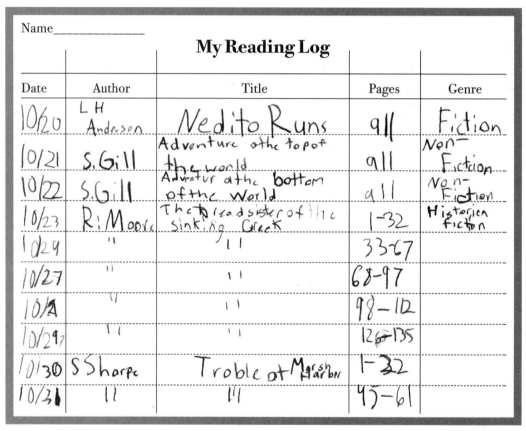

My Reading Log

Name_____

Date	Author	Title	Pages	Genre
10/20	L H Andersen	Nedito Runs	all	Fiction
10/21	S. Gill	Adventure at the top of the world	all	Non-Fiction
10/22	S. Gill	Adventur at the bottom of the World	all	Non-Fiction
10/23	R. Moore	The head sister of the sinking Creek	1-32	Historian Fiction
10/24	''	''	33-67	
10/27	''	''	68-97	
10/28	''	''	98-12	
10/29	''	''	126-135	
10/30	S Sharpe	Troble at Marsh Harbor	1-32	
10/31	''	''	45-61	

Other record-keeping tasks students are responsible for include signing up for conferences, listing completed response projects, and, in book club situations, assigning and recording reading and written follow ups.

In the writing workshop, students also have a variety of record-keeping responsibilities, which include keeping track of writing engaged in and reporting whether a piece is completed to the publication stage (not all are). Students also record various mechanical skills that they have mastered during the year, which are usually pointed out to students during conferences with the teacher (see Appendix, Form 11). As with reading, students take the initiative for requesting writing conferences and making sure they have a clear purpose.

We have found that two keys to effective student record keeping are modeling and organization. Before students are asked to take responsibility for the simplest record-keeping task, teachers should model the process several times and then follow up throughout the year with one or two focus lessons and reviews of record-keeping procedures. Organizational tools for record keeping also help students to maintain accurate records: two-pocket folders or three-ring binders work, depending on preference. Whatever the system, experience has proven that simpler is better.

Student-, Peer-, and Self-Evaluation

The workshop approach provides for and requires a great deal of student self-reflection and evaluation. Students are given clear guidelines and expectations and then are asked to evaluate how well they achieved their intended purposes (see Appendix, Forms 8, 12, and 13). When writing, students regularly record observations and thoughts, an activity that allows them to think like writers. In order to organize these seemingly unconnected observations and thoughts, students are given time on a regular basis to review their notebooks for ideas about themes. Once they have reflected on their writing and discovered connections between the various entries, students are ready to develop a piece of writing.

When students complete a piece of writing, they are asked to engage in self-evaluation by comparing their written work with a predetermined set of descriptors or rubric. We use writing scoring guidelines based on state standards (see Appendix, Form 14). The writing scoring guidelines include descriptors for focus, content, organization, style, and conventions and is based on a four-point scale. During focus lessons throughout the year, we provide samples of student writing and then, as a class, evaluate the pieces against the criteria in the rubric. Students also use the rubrics in peer conferences. When we evaluate or grade student writing, we use a format that incorporates the rubric descriptors and scoring system.

During the reading strand of the workshop, self-evaluation also occurs in several ways. When students complete a reading response, we evaluate the response using a Reading Project Evaluation (see Appendix, Form 9) (Jackson, 1992). This form is particularly effective because it provides a section where students are asked to reflect on their projects and write about the positive and negative aspects and what they learned.

When students participate in book clubs, a great deal of metacognition takes place. As they read their books, students are asked to write down any thoughts or questions that the story brings to mind. Lucy Calkins (1995) suggests providing each student with a package of sticky notes to use for recording ideas during reading. When students meet for their book discussion, these notes provide the beginnings of their conversation. Periodically, students are also asked to evaluate the functioning of their book clubs, for example, "How well do we work together?" This is useful for us as well as for the students, as it provides possible topics to be addressed in focus lessons or on an individual basis.

Teacher Record Keeping

There is no doubt that the workshop approach requires more record keeping than the "traditional" approach to language arts. However, through experimentation, we are confident that each teacher can find a system that works for him or her.

Teachers keep records of many of the same things the students do—books read, projects completed, writings in progress, and skills developed and mastered. Included in the Appendix are a variety of forms that can be used "as is" or adapted to suit a specific purpose or style.

One important component of record keeping that is the sole responsibility of the teacher is the notetaking after a teacher-student conference (see Figure 11). The format we use provides space for notes about what

FIGURE 11
READING WORKSHOP CONFERENCE

Reading Workshop Conference

Name _____

Date	Book	Comments	Goals for next conference
5/15	Poppy (AVI)	3/4 of the way finished - good re-telling of events up to this point. Thinking about using this book for May response project.	Complete Poppy by 5/19 and decide on book for project.
5/19	"	Goal met - Poppy completed. Book response begun - Rough draft in T.J. response log. Would like to make a character map for project. Wants to read Poppy and Rye next.	Have sketch of character map finished and written response ready for editing by 5/24.

occurred in the conference and a separate entry for the student's goal for the next conference meeting. The conference notes are kept in a binder–notes for each student along with response-project records and writing evaluations. Whether for reading or writing, conference notes are an extremely important part of record keeping and can provide the basis for assessment and evaluation.

Teacher-Initiated Assessment and Evaluation

Once again, it is important to reiterate how crucial assessment and evaluation are to the teaching-learning cycle–especially in a workshop classroom. The workshop approach offers teachers opportunities for frequent and meaningful assessment and evaluation of their students. Teachers who take advantage of these opportunities will be able to tailor their planning and teaching to meet the needs of all their students more successfully, while engendering a spirit of community among the learners in their classrooms.

Short and Harste (1996) cite field notes as the heart of good teaching. Teachers utilizing a workshop approach should observe and record their students' activities and progress in both formal and informal settings. Students sign up for formal conferences as the need arises, and they come with a goal in mind. The conferences are structured, and discussions in these conferences can address individual needs, but also may give rise to whole-class or small-group focus lessons. When not involved in formal conferences, teachers can sit down with a student as he is reading or writing and informally "chat" (no longer than 1 or 2 minutes) about the student's work. These chats often can provide insight into a student's self-perception of himself as a reader and writer.

Interest and attitude surveys are also wonderful tools for assessing student perceptions and needs. We try to administer different surveys throughout the year in order to develop a continuum of student and class attitudes (see Appendix, Form 11). To help develop your own survey,

Lucy Calkins (1991) offers the following statements as examples for learning about children's "lifelines" (personal life experiences) as readers and writers:

> As a writer, I....
>
> As a reader, I....
>
> In this workshop, I hope that we....
>
> If you're going to respond well to my writing (or reading), you need to know....
>
> My greatest fear as a writer (reader) is....
>
> One thing you still may not know about me as a writer (reader) is....
>
> My ambition as a writer (or reader) is to.... (p. 18)

Donald Graves (1994) characterizes the teacher as a "learning historian," and he offers a three-column exercise that teachers can use to begin their journeys as historians (see Figure 12, page 34). A few weeks after the beginning of school, the teacher makes a list of each student's name, from memory, in the first column. In the next column, again from memory, the teacher lists an interest or experience that she associates with each student. In the third column, the teacher notes whether she has confirmed or acknowledged the experience or interest with the child. For example, "Gee, Jimmy, you sure know an awful lot about snakes!" This simple act of confirmation begins to make students aware of their own "effective learning history." Graves also cites the importance to students of being known by the teacher—being aware that the teacher has specific information about a student helps that student to learn.

As stated in this chapter, we use a holistic approach for evaluating student writing that involves a rubric of specific criteria supported by consistency and modeling. From the first day of school, we talk about and refer to writing rubrics in focus lessons, conferences, and whole-class activities. Students learn the language of the rubric and become evaluators them-

FIGURE 12
THREE-COLUMN EXERCISE

Three-Column Exercise

October

Name	Special Interest	Acknowledged
Andrew	Friend to the underdog	✓
Amy	Photography	✓ (Yearbook)
Chris	Fan of Roald Dahl	✓
Shane	Skateboarding	✓ (All About Me)
Devon	Horse back riding	✓
Casey	N-Sync maniac	✓ (Gave her poster)
Molly	Acting	✓ (Musical?)
Kurt	? Need to investigate	
Colin	Sports	✓
Dan F.	Sign language – Hearing impaired brother	✓ (Conference)
Dan H.	Animals	✓ (Fish feeder)
Jessic J.	Mom from England	✓
Kelly	Crafty things	✓
Lauren F.	Foster brother	✓ (All about me)

selves. We have developed a simple writing scoring guide that is attached to those pieces of writing that are "graded" (see Appendix, Form 13).

Students' reading response projects are evaluated similarly to their writing. At the beginning of the year, time is spent discussing and modeling the various criteria that are used to evaluate student-response projects. Expectations are clearly stated and sample projects are shared. After students finish each project, they receive the completed Reading Project Evaluation, which they use for self-reflection and share with their parents. We keep track of the number and types of responses completed by each student, as well as the evaluation score for each project.

A more formal way to assess students on a regular basis is by using the running-record process, which provides a quick analysis of the types of errors or miscues students make when reading aloud. This process is based on the three types of cues good readers use to help them comprehend written material—semantic, visual, or syntactic. While a student reads aloud either from a text of choice or one that the teacher chooses, the teacher records any mistakes or miscues made by the student. Later, the teacher analyzes each miscue and determines the category into which it falls. After the running record is completed, we often ask the student to orally retell the story's main points in order to assess comprehension as well. For more detailed descriptions of procedures for taking and analyzing running records, see *Practical Assessments* by Adele Fiderer (1995), and *An Observational Survey of Early Literacy Achievement* by Marie Clay (1993).

The significance and value of assessment and evaluation cannot be overstated. All of our planning and teaching revolves around the information obtained through these methods. To make the workshop approach work effectively, each teacher must experiment and investigate until he or she finds a system (or systems) for assessment and evaluation that is manageable, provides appropriate information, and helps to meet the needs of all students.

4

Putting It All Together:
The Workshop in Action

W orkshop classrooms come in all sizes and shapes. The variety of models we have seen are too numerous to count. The important thing to remember when reviewing the different workshop models presented here is that the most effective model is the one that reflects the strengths and needs of the individual classroom.

Time Frames

Generally, the workshop is best implemented when large blocks of time are available. In most cases presented here, teachers had approximately 2 to 2½ hours per day for language arts instruction, in which, in addition to reading and writing workshops, they included time for spelling and phonics instruction, read-alouds, and guided or whole-group instruction using an anthology or novel.

The majority of the actual workshop time is devoted to students' writing and reading. The independent writing and reading period ranges from 30 to 45 minutes per workshop session. Independent reading and writing includes activities such as reading silently, partner reading, creating reading responses, writing in notebooks, participating in peer response groups, and participating in peer editing conferences. While students are engaged in these tasks, the teacher meets with other students, either individually or in small groups. It is during these meetings or conferences that teachers can provide individualized direct instruction, small-group guided-reading practice, and supervised peer-writing practice, or conduct student assessment. This directed student-teacher interaction is probably one of the most beneficial aspects of the workshop approach. Teachers are free to meet the needs of all students and to provide support for struggling readers and writers, and enrichment opportunities for competent readers and writers.

Focus lessons and student sharing take up approximately 10 to 15 minutes of the workshop. Focus lessons can be held separately for reading and writing, or a combined lesson can be held on a topic that is relevant to both. Some teachers use their class read-aloud book as a springboard for introducing focus lessons. For instance, the teacher might introduce a specific strategy during read-aloud and encourage students to think about this strategy during independent reading. The class could then come back to this strategy during sharing time later that day. (See Chapter 5 for suggestions and strategies for developing meaningful focus lessons related to curricular and standards-based goals.)

Schedules

There are many different and effective ways to schedule the workshop into the teaching day. Some teachers schedule one large block of time for all language activities, while others schedule several components throughout the day. Following are five sample schedules with brief descriptions of how each fits into the whole school day. You may follow one of these schedules or adapt one to fit your own time constraints and personal preferences. The key is to set up the workshop so that you and your students feel comfortable and relaxed with the process.

One schedule is that of a third-grade teacher in a school that subscribes to the Four Blocks method of instruction and the use of an anthology series (Figure 13). Notice the extremely structured approach to the language arts curriculum and how it is broken down into very discrete parts. A criticism of this particular schedule might be the limited time

FIGURE 13
FOUR BLOCKS METHOD

Monday	Tuesday	Wednesday	Thursday	Friday
Read-Aloud Library language arts Book exchange	Phonemic awareness/ Working with words Listening skills	Phonemic awareness/ Working with words Listening skills	Phonemic awareness Working with words Listening skills	Sparkle (a spelling game) Spelling review game Read-aloud
New spelling and vocabulary words New story Predict Picture walk	Computer lab Working on skills Language arts folders for each theme	Writing on a topic related to the week's story Brainstorm Rough draft Editing	Specific skill work Partners read story of the week/ Small-group reading	Spelling test Reading workshop Share time
Read-aloud Book talk Skills covered by the new story	Specific skill work Reader's workshop for skill Share time	Conference Revising Good copies	Letter tiles Spelling Bingo Spelling review	Teach and Share presentations

given to writing. This teacher is not yet comfortable with allowing students to write about topics of their own choosing.

For another third-grade schedule, the teacher has provided a key that codes each activity with a series of district curricular objectives (see Figure 14, p. 40). This teacher also is working within the framework of a Four Blocks structure with an anthology series, but she gives students more opportunity for independent reading and writing, while at the same time exposing them to direct instruction through the anthology and focus lessons.

The final third-grade schedule provides the opportunity to see the progress made throughout a whole day (see Figure 15, page 40). Notice that this teacher includes a short but specific phonics component daily in addition to time designated for guided reading in small groups.

FIGURE 14
THIRD-GRADE SCHEDULE WITH CURRICULAR OBJECTIVES

Language Arts Framework/High-Average/Accelerated Reading Group
   1 - shared/guided reading
   2 - self-selected reading
   3 - writing
   4 - speaking/listening
   5 - working with words

Monday
   2 - library - self-selected book exchange
   5 - working with words - spelling words for the week
                         - including words spelled incorrectly on past tests

Monday through Thursday (at least once a week)
   1 - direct reading instruction - usually with anthology
   1 - add vocabulary words to word wall and vocab books
   1 - partner reading - usually with books
      3 - comprehension questions/writing activities
   3 - free-writing journal - including sentence edit

Monday through Thursday (at least twice a week)
   Minilessons: 1 - reading skills
                3 - writing skills
   2 - reading workshop
      3 - reading logs/reading workshop notebook - summaries or generic questions

Thursday
Computer lab:
   3 - word processing/editing/skill practice activities/ final copies
   1 - Accelerated Reader/Star Reader

Friday
   5 - spelling review/test
      3 - including sentence dictation with high frequency words or sentence edit
   4 - Sharing time:
      free writing journal/stories/reading workshop notebook

FIGURE 15
THIRD-GRADE WHOLE-DAY SCHEDULE

9:00 — 9:15	Power Phonics Minilessons on vowel combinations using poetry and rhymes.
9:15 — 10:15	Guided Reading (Flexible small groups focusing on skill development. Other students work independently on small-group reading and language activities.)
10:15 — 10:30	Read-aloud/Snack (Read aloud to class books that are two grade levels above third grade.)
10:30 — 11:30	Writing Workshop
11:30 — 12:15	Reading Workshop (Students read book on independent reading level while teacher holds individual conferences.)
12:15 — 1:00	Lunch
1:00 — 2:00	Math
2:00 — 3:00	Social Studies/Science

The fourth-grade schedule provides a much looser framework, but includes specific time allotments (see Figure 16, page 42). Note that specific opportunities are provided for the teaching of skills in small- and large-group settings and for the needed independent practice every day.

The fifth-grade class schedule illustrates a day from beginning to end (see Figure 17, page 42). In this school, the language arts program is entirely literature based and literacy centered, and this teacher addresses phonics through the district-developed spelling program. Some students in this classroom are reading significantly below level and have identified learning disabilities. Note that specific time is allotted during each reading workshop period for small-group direct instruction. These groups are flexible and include no more than four students at any given time.

FIGURE 16
FOURTH-GRADE SCHEDULE

9:00 — 9:10	Focus Lesson Wwriting
9:10 — 9:40	Writing—journals/book projects/other
9:40 — 10:10	Working With Words (spelling/vocabulary)
10:10 — 11:10	Anthology/Novels (whole-group and small-group instruction)
11:10 — 11:40	Reading Workshop (independent reading and conferences)

FIGURE 17
FIFTH-GRADE SCHEDULE—LITERACY CENTERED

9:00 – 10:00	Math
10:00 – 11:30	Language Arts instruction novels (whole class/book clubs) spelling (phonics-based patterns) vocabulary study
11:30 – 12:15	Reading Workshop focus lessons independent self-selected reading conferences small-group direct instruction (three times per week) project work sharing
12:15 – 1:00	Lunch
1:00 – 1:15	Read-aloud
1:15 – 2:00	Writing Workshop focus lessons independent writing peer/teacher conferences publishing sharing
2:00 – 2:45	Social Studies/Science
2:45 – 3:25	Special Area Class

Management Techniques

The workshop framework allows students to make choices in their learning and to work independently in order to meet goals. However, this freedom does not mean that workshop classes are chaotic. On the contrary, workshop teachers must be masters of classroom management. Every student is working toward a goal, and the teacher must stay aware of this. The teacher meets with each student on a regular basis and keeps track of what occurs in these conferences. Assessment occurs frequently. A method must be developed for using this information to inform instruction. Progress reports must reflect all that occurs within the workshop, and it is up to the teacher to develop an accurate method of tracking and reporting progress. There are many and varied techniques a teacher can employ to ensure that the workshop runs smoothly and efficiently. Listed are five techniques that we have seen used effectively as tools for managing various aspects of the workshop. We stress again that only by experimentation can a teacher find the method that works best for him and his students.

1. Status of the Class: This is a 5-minute survey taken at the beginning of each workshop in which the teacher determines what each student will be working on during that particular session. Students enter each session with a purpose.

2. Clothespin Method (see Figure 18, page 44): This is particularly effective for younger students. The teacher creates a chart with each aspect of the workshop listed (ie., independent reading/ writing, conferencing, editing, and book response). Students each have a clothespin with their name on it. At the beginning of each workshop period, students clip their pin to the component they will be working on that day. As students move from one component to another, they move their clothespins. This provides a quick, visual summary for the teacher and gives students concrete reminders of goals and tasks.

FIGURE 18
CLOTHESPIN CHART

Choose a Book	Read That Book
Conference	**Reading Response Journal**
Creative Response Project	**Share**

3. Record-Keeping Forms: In most workshops, students share the responsibility for record keeping. Students keep workshop folders in which they track the status of writing projects and their progress with reading goals. The teacher keeps similar records with the addition of anecdotal notes from conferences and small-group sessions. As mentioned earlier, a class chart on which student goals are posted is a quick way to track what each student is working on (see Appendix, Forms 1–7, and 14).

4. Conference Schedules and Sign-Ups: Conferences can be difficult to schedule, so a commitment must be made to hold conferences during each session. Depending on the age of students and the teacher's preference, specific conference schedules can be developed and posted, or students may sign up for conferences on an as-needed basis (see Appendix, Form 3). Whichever method is chosen, it is important that students meet with the teacher on a regular basis—they cannot be allowed to "fall through the cracks."

5. Student-Sharing Schedules: Student sharing also should occur on a regular basis; however, it should not overtake the workshop. Many teachers find it particularly helpful to designate specific sharing days and specific students to share on each day.

Expectations for Students

In workshop classrooms, students spend much of their time working independently. They continually work toward goals they develop in collaboration with the teacher. Goals may be big or small, but students understand that they will be held accountable for making steady progress toward each goal. Students also understand that reading and writing are like other subjects in school, ones in which they will not do well if they do not use time wisely and work toward completion of goals. We have found it helpful to have student expectations actually posted in the classroom so there is never a doubt as to what students are responsible for completing (see Figure 19, page 46).

FIGURE 19
READING WORKSHOP REQUIREMENTS

1. Complete a minimum of one letter a week in literature log.

2. Attend one teacher conference every 2 weeks.

3. Complete one activity per week.

4. Complete one book club review per book.

5. Complete one Self-Evaluation of Reading - entrance conference.

6. Complete one Am I Developing as a Reader? - exit conference.

Reading Goals

In addition to individual goals set during conferences, many teachers set specific class goals of either number of pages or books read (see Appendix, Forms 1 and 2). Generally, teachers set monthly reading goals. For example, in our fifth-grade class, the goal was to complete three books each month. If a student was reading a particularly long or challenging book, the goal would be modified accordingly. Another goal was to complete one book response each month. Students had a choice of books to which they would respond. Both book and response goals accounted for a portion of each student's reading grade for each marking period.

Another goal-setting method for reading involves the use of bookmarks. Each student uses two bookmarks—a start bookmark and a goal bookmark. Students place the start bookmark on the page where they begin reading, and they place the goal bookmark on the page they would like to reach by the end of the session. The teacher periodically discusses the bookmark goals with each student in order to determine the success of this tool for the student. This system is particularly helpful in developing time-management skills and in meeting class reading goals.

Writing Goals

As with reading, the teacher must establish specific classroom goals for writing projects (see Appendix, Forms 12 and 13). These goals may revolve around completion of writing projects, or they may relate to specific aspects of written work. In our fifth-grade class, the goal was to complete one writing project monthly, along with specific rubric-related activities. Completed writing projects can take many forms and need not be stories or essays. Additionally, some teachers choose to combine reading and writing during some months, focusing on written response to literature.

A Word About Leveling

As discussed in Chapter 2, when implementing a reading workshop approach, it is extremely beneficial for teachers to arrange their classroom libraries according to reading levels. Initially, the task of leveling books takes time and may seem daunting. However, in the long run, a leveled classroom library is an invaluable tool in ensuring that each student chooses books that are at his independent reading level.

How do we accurately determine the reading level of books? There are many resources available to aid in determining reading levels: computer programs, packaged systems such as Accelerated Reader (Advantage Learning System, no date), and published summaries and lists of leveled books. There are entire books devoted to the topic of leveling books (Fountas & Pinnell, 1999; Routman, 1994; Weaver, 2000). Ideally, the leveling of books occurs as a schoolwide initiative, however, individual teachers may undertake this task on their own. Once a system for leveling has been determined, parent volunteers can be quite helpful in completing the job.

Once books are assigned levels, how do we organize the library to reflect this? A variety of methods may be employed. Books may be labeled with the actual grade-level designation. Books may be leveled with letters such as A, B, C, D, which reflect segments of reading levels. A broader organizational system uses labels of *easy*, *medium*, and *hard*. In our fifth-grade class, we not only labeled by reading level, but also by genre, because having students read a variety of genres was an important goal to us. Whatever system is developed, the reading level of the book must be easily recognizable to students so that they may make appropriate choices for their independent reading.

Focus Lessons

As discussed in previous chapters, focus lessons play a crucial role in workshop classrooms. In addition to individual conferences, focus lessons are a key to providing individualized instruction. It is during these brief lessons that the class's specific strengths and needs can be addressed, along with particular curricular and standards-based objectives. Students learn how to be good readers and writers because they are taught the strategies that good readers and writers use and are given significant amounts of time to practice those strategies. Focus lessons provide the teaching opportunity. Independent reading and writing provide the time for students to practice the strategies.

Developing Focus Lessons

Most important, focus lessons should address specifically the students' needs as readers and writers. Focus lessons should have a genuine purpose if we are to expect students to put the lesson material into practice. We have found that focus lessons are most effective when they concentrate on one topic or skill. Trying to cover too much material in a 15-minute lesson can be overwhelming for teachers and students.

Generally, we categorized focus lessons into three types: procedural, literary, and strategies and skills (Atwell, 1998). For obvious reasons, procedural focus lessons are most common at the beginning of the year and are used to model the various roles and tasks in the workshop and to set clear expectations. We modeled almost every aspect of the workshop, often having students role play different tasks during the lessons.

FIGURE 20
DESCRIPTIVE PHRASES

Descriptive phrases   10/23/00

She ~ Rachel

① underneath the years / ② cry like you're
3 years ③ growing old like wooden dolls,
onion, tree rings / ④ 11 years like pennies
rattling in a 10 bandade box. / ⑤ sleeves like jumprope
⑥ sweater seems 1,000 years old / ⑦ little
voice like 4 years old / ⑧ sweater sits
like a mountain on desk. / ⑨ sweater
hangs on the edge of desk like waterfall
⑩ sweater smells like cottage cheese /
⑪ body shaking like hicupps / ⑫ far
away like a tiny balloon.) ⑬ Wish you
were 102 to be able to say something
⑭ 11, she was speechless. / ⑮ Wishes
that sweater would be so small,
you have to squint your eyes
to see it.

Although this may seem tedious and time consuming, it proved to be a key element in the success of the workshop throughout the remainder of the year.

When planning focus lessons, we took into account the student needs that we saw within the framework of the workshop, and we tried to integrate curricular needs as well. For instance, during a writing-workshop poetry exploration, we noticed that many students were using descriptive language ineffectively. One of our grade-level objectives was to introduce the use of imagery in creative writing, which was a natural tie-in. We developed a focus lesson using a powerful short story "Eleven" (Cisneros, 1991) as the basis for a discussion of descriptive language and imagery as tools for evoking strong emotions in a reader. Students were directed to listen for strong descriptive phrases in the story. One student recorded many phrases for future discussion and, perhaps, use in her own writing (see Figure 20). Another benefit of this lesson was the obvious connection between reading and writing made by using a piece of literature to discuss a writing strategy.

Another successful method of developing meaningful topics for focus lessons involved the entire school faculty brainstorming a common list of important reading comprehension strategies to be taught (see Figure 21, page 52). The faculty also generated a reminder list of how to teach students to decode unfamiliar words. Not every student needs the same lesson from this list at the same time. However, if you do conduct whole-class lessons, they can serve as good reviews for some students and as introductions for others. At times, you also might choose to present focus lessons in small-group settings to those students who are ready for a particular strategy.

Many schools and states now have specific sets of standards in place for language arts. These standards provide a wealth of topics for focus lessons, which can be used to introduce students to and instruct them on the skills and strategies they must acquire in order to achieve the given standards. The activity period of each workshop gives students the time to

FIGURE 21
INTERMEDIATE READING STRATEGIES

What Good Readers Do

Before Reading:
- Preview   Title, headings, pictures, charts
- Predict   What will the author say?
- Ask   What questions may be answered?
- Tell   What do I already know?
- Think   Why am I reading this?

During Reading:
- Visualize   Make pictures in your mind.
- Predict   What will come next?
- Summarize   What did the author say?
- Question   Make up questions about what I am reading.
- Clarify   What was not clear?

  If I don't understand, if the story doesn't match with what I know, or if my mind was wandering, I can
  - —keep reading to try to make sense.
  - —go back and reread.
  - —slow down my rate of reading.

After Reading:
- Summarize   What did I read?
- Reread   What didn't I understand?
- Check   Did I make good predictions?
- Apply   How does the story fit with what I know?
- Think   What have I learned?

practice and refine these skills. The conferences allow teachers the opportunity to assess and evaluate student progress toward meeting the standards.

Tailoring focus lessons to the needs of the class is appropriate; however, this does not mean that new sets of focus lessons must be developed each year. We found lesson files to be particularly effective, and after a few years, we developed an extensive collection. Although we prefer to develop our own lessons and accompanying materials, other workshop teachers employ commercial materials as the basis of each focus lesson. There are several sources that can provide material for both skills-and-strategies and literary lessons. For instance, the program "Writers Express" (Elsholz, Kemper, Nathan, & Sebranek, 2000) includes teacher handbooks that provide easy-to-use workshop lessons that may be of assistance to teachers who are struggling with focus lessons.

Finally, many professional resources are available to help teachers generate ideas for focus lessons: *In the Middle* (Atwell, 1998), *Craft Lessons* (Fletcher, 1998), and *Readers' Workshop* (Hagerty, 1992). The most important thing to remember when choosing lessons to share with the class is that the needs of the class should drive the choices we make. Meeting the needs of the students within the framework of the curricular standards is the ultimate goal of all our workshop components, and toward that end, the focus lesson provides valuable instructional time.

Final Thoughts

Throughout the implementation of the workshop framework, the ultimate goal has been to provide the means and time to address fully the needs of each student. We are strongly committed to this approach because of the observed measurable results—increases in reading and writing skills—and, perhaps more important, the results that are somewhat harder to measure—increased interest in and desire to read and write. As we have shown through conference records, student samples, and teacher feedback, workshop classrooms are literacy-centered classrooms. Students voluntarily and spontaneously engage in discussions about their reading and writing on a regular basis. Reading and writing are no longer viewed as school skills, but life skills.

There are many research-grounded supports for using a workshop approach. To summarize the many benefits discussed in this book, using a reading-writing workshop

- allows teachers to meet individual student needs,
- provides time and context for frequent and regular assessment,
- addresses standards and curricular goals in a meaningful fashion,
- corresponds with the teaching-learning cycle, and
- provides a framework for teaching specific skills and the opportunity for extended practice with feedback on a regular basis.

The workshop gave us the needed framework to teach in a manner that was most effective for our students. You may choose a model similar to ours, or you may try some components and modify others to meet the needs of your particular students. Whatever the case, remember that teaching is not a one-size-fits-all endeavor. The more we do to individualize instruction, the more successful our students will be.

Sample Assessment and Record-Keeping Forms

Forms for Reading Workshop

FORM 1

Name _____				

My Reading Log

Date	Author	Title	Pages	Genre

FORM 2

Reading Record
(for younger students)

Name _____

Title	Author	Date

FORM 3

Reading Conference Sign-Up Sheet

Name	Date	For What Purpose?	Complete

FORM 4

Reading Workshop Conference: Anecdotal Notes

Name _____

Date	Book	Comments	Goals for next conference

FORM 5

Reading Workshop Conference: Assessment Notes

Student's name _____ Date _____

Title of book/fiction-nonfiction _____

Pages read aloud _____

Before Reading

1. Why did you choose this book? _____

2. Is it an **easy**, **just right** or **challenging** book? Why do you think so? _____

_____

3. What did you do before you started to read this book? _____

_____

During Reading + = Behavior observed	
Self-corrects	
Re-reads to clarify meaning	
Sounds out to decode words	
Slows down when reading difficult text	
Substitutes familiar words/makes meaningful substitutions	
Understands vocabulary	
Reads confidently	
Speaks clearly	
Uses picture clues appropriately	
Teacher's Notes	

After Reading − = Not proficient ✔ = developing ✔⁺ = proficient	
Identifies setting	
Identifies main characters	
Summarizes key points	
Retells sequence accurately	
Predicts what will happen next	
Questions	
Teacher's Notes	

FORM 6

Reading Workshop Conference: Skills Checklist

Name _____ Date _____   Name _____ Date _____

Title _____   Title _____

Work attack _____   Work attack _____

Fluency_____   Fluency_____

Expression _____   Expression _____

Can answer detailed questions about the story _____   Can answer detailed questions about the story _____

Can retell the story_____   Can retell the story_____

Can define words from the story _____   Can define words from the story _____

Comments: Comments:

Name _____ Date _____   Name _____ Date _____

Title _____   Title _____

Work attack _____   Work attack _____

Fluency_____   Fluency_____

Expression _____   Expression _____

Can answer detailed questions about the story _____   Can answer detailed questions about the story _____

Can retell the story_____   Can retell the story_____

Can define words from the story _____   Can define words from the story _____

Comments: Comments:

Key:	O = Outstanding	S = Satisfactory	N= Needs strengthening
	I = Showing improvement	* = Adapted	NA = Not applicable

FORM 7

Teacher's Conference Record Sheet

Student's Name _____

Date	Title/Book	(Things done well) Conference Discussion	Things to Improve (Teacher Notes)

FORM 8

Personal Response Rubric

	Student	Teacher
Response begins with a topic sentence that restates the question or main idea.		
There are 7 to 10 sentences that give enough detail and examples to make the ideas clear and complete.		
Sentences are complete—no fragments or run-ons.		
No words have been repeated or left out.		
Sentences have been properly punctuated or capitalized.		
This journal response reflects thoughtfulness and effort.		

FORM 9

Reading Project Evaluation

Name _____ Date _____

Project _____ Score _____ / 30 pts.

The following scale is based on performance expectations for most 3rd graders.

1 = Unsatisfactory   2 = Below Expectations   3 = Meets Expectations
4 = Exceeds Expectations   5 = Clearly Outstanding

1. Development   The project follows a logical order and has enough information to clearly present the ideas.

    1   2   3   4   5

2. Following Directions   Specific directions for assignment were followed.

    1   2   3   4   5

3. Mechanics   Capital letters and ending punctuation have been used correctly. Words appropriate for 3rd graders have been spelled properly. Ideas are presented in complete sentences.

    1   2   3   4   5

4. Visual Aids   All visual aids are appropriate. They are neat and show detail to completely express the idea.

    1   2   3   4   5

5. General Appearance   The project is neat and complete.

    1   2   3   4   5

6. Creativity   The project reflects a new idea.

    1   2   3   4   5

Teacher Comments:_____

_____

Student Reflections:_____

I did well with _____

I could improve _____

My goal for the next project is _____

Forms for Writing Workshop

FORM 10

Writing Checklist

Name _____

Date	Topic/Theme	Stage of Process	Comments

FORM 11

As a Writer...

I am beginning to...	I usually...

FORM 12

Writing Skills Criteria Rubric

1 = weak
2 = developing or adequate
3 = strong

This piece of writing:

Expresses ideas that are clear and easy to understand _____

Supports basically one main idea that develops a mood or feeling _____

Is broken down into separate paragraphs _____

Has enough supporting information, details, and examples _____

Has no run-ons or fragments _____

Does not repeat the same word or phrase frequently _____

Uses the same verb tense throughout _____

Contains no grammar or usage errors—nor awkward phrasing _____

Shows evidence of higher level vocabulary or purposeful word choice _____

Accurate spelling _____

Correct punctuation _____

Comments:

FORM 13

Writing Scoring Guide

Mechanics

1. Capitalization/Punctuation	1	2	3
2. Sentences–No fragments/Run-ons	1	2	3
3. Verb tense agreement/Correct grammar	1	2	3
4. Paragraphs–defined, 5–8 sentences	1	2	3

Organization and Style

1. Logical order of ideas/sequence	1	2	3
2. Complete development of ideas	1	2	3
3. Ideas clearly expressed and easily understood	1	2	3

Focus Areas

1. Contains details to support ideas	1	2	3
2. Descriptive words and phrases used	1	2	3
3. Personal feelings and reactions are expressed	1	2	3

Key:

1 = Expectation not met

2 = Expectation successfully met

3 = Exceeds expectation

FORM 14

Writing Scoring Guidelines

Focus: Do you stick to the topic?   1   2   3   4

Content: Do you use examples and details to develop
            your ideas?   1   2   3   4

Organization: Are your ideas in logical order? Do you
            have an introduction and conclusion?   1   2   3   4

Style: Have you used strong words? Do you vary the
        length and type of sentences?   1   2   3   4

Conventions: Have you used correct grammar,
           punctuation, and spelling?   1   2   3   4

Total Points: _____/20

Name:_____Period: _____

Assignment:_____Date: _____

Comments:

References

Advantage Learning System. (no date). *Accelerated reader*. Wisconsin Rapids, WI: Author.

Atwell, N. (1998). *In the middle: New understandings about reading, writing, and learning* (2nd ed.). Portsmouth, NH: Boynton/Cook.

Calkins, L.M. (1991). *Living between the lines*. Portsmouth, NH: Heinemann.

Calkins, L.M. (1994). *The art of teaching writing*. Portsmouth, NH: Heinemann.

Calkins, L.M. (1995, February). *Re-imagining the reading/writing workshop*. Baltimore: Heinemann Professional Workshop.

Cisneros, S. (1991). *Woman hollering creek*. New York: Random House.

Clay, M. (1993). *An observation survey of early literacy achievement*. Portsmouth, NH: Heinemann.

Cole, R. (Ed.). (1995). *Educating everybody's children: Diverse teaching strategies for diverse learners (what research and practice say about improving achievement)*. Alexandria, VA: Association for Supervision and Curriculum Development.

Cunningham, P., Hall, D., & Sigmon, C.M. (1999). *The teacher's guide to the four blocks*. Greensboro, NC: Carson-Dellosa.

Education Department of Western Australia. (1994). *Reading developmental continuum*. East Perth, Western Australia: Addison Wesley Longman.

Education Department of Western Australia. (1994). *Reading resource book*. East Perth, Western Australia: Addison Wesley Longman.

Eggleton, J., & Windsor J. (1995). *Linking the language strands*. Auckland, New Zealand: Wings.

Elsholz, C., Kemper, D., Nathan, R., & Sebranek, P. (2000). *Writers express*. Wilmington, MA: Great Source Educational Group.

Fiderer, A. (1995). *Practical assessments for literature-based reading classrooms*. New York: Scholastic.

Fletcher, R., & Portalupi, J. (1998). *Craft lessons*. York, ME: Stenhouse.

Fountas, I.C., & Pinnell, G.S. (1999). *Matching books to readers: Using leveled books in guided reading, K–3*. Portsmouth, NH: Heinemann.

Gambrell, L.B., & Almasi, J.F. (1996). *Lively discussions! Fostering engaged reading*. Newark, DE: International Reading Association.

Gardner, H. (1993). *Multiple intelligences*. New York: Basic Books.

Graves, D.H. (1991). *Build a literate classroom*. Portsmouth, NH: Heinemann.

Graves, D.H. (1994). *A fresh look at writing*. Portsmouth, NH: Heinemann.

Graves, D.H. (1996, March). *Putting writing to work across the curriculum*. Philadelphia: Heinemann Professional Workshop.

Griffin, E. (1994, November). *Developmentally appropriate practices*. Chadds Ford, PA: Griffin Center for Professional Development.

Hagerty, P. (1992). *Readers' workshop*. Richmond Hill, Ontario, Canada: Scholastic Canada.

Jackson, N.R. (1992). *The reading-writing workshop: Getting started*. New York: Scholastic Professional.

Kovalik, S. (1995). *How to make your classroom brain-compatible* (Cassette Recording No. 95-3210). Alexandria, VA: Association for Supervision and Curriculum Development.

Martinez, M.G., & Roser, N.L. (Eds.). (1995). *Book talk and beyond: Children and teachers respond to literature*. Newark, DE: International Reading Association.

Ministry of Education, Wellington, New Zealand. (1997). *Reading for life: The learner as a reader*. Katonah, NY: Richard C. Owens.

National Reading Panel. (2000). *Report of the National Reading Panel: Teaching children to read*. Bethesda, MD: Author.

Roller, C.M. (1996). *Variability not disability: Struggling readers in a workshop classroom*. Newark, DE: International Reading Association.

Routman, R. (1994). *The blue pages: Resources for teachers from invitations: Changing as teachers and learners K–12*. Portsmouth, NH: Heinemann.

Short, K.G., & Harste, J.C. (1996). *Creating classrooms for authors and inquirers*. Portsmouth, NH: Heinemann.

Weaver, B.W. (2000). *Leveling books K–6: Matching readers to text*. Newark, DE: International Reading Association.

ADDITIONAL PROFESSIONAL READING

Armstrong, T. (1994). *Multiple intelligences in the classroom*. Alexandria, VA: Association for Supervision and Curriculum Development.

Batzel, J. (1992). *Portfolio assessment and evaluation*. Cypress, CA: Creative Teaching Press.

Chapman, C. (1993). *If the shoe fits....* Palatine, IL: IRI/Skylight.

Robb, L. (1996). *Reading strategies that work*. New York: Scholastic Professional.

RESOURCES FOR CLASSROOM BOOK COLLECTIONS

Learning Links
  thematic collections
  author collections
Richard C. Owen
  beginning readers
  short stories for reluctant and advanced older readers
Rigby
  beginning readers
  short story collections for older readers
Scholastic
  all levels
  thematic collections
  computer-based "Wiggle Works" and "Smart Books" programs

RESOURCES FOR RESPONSE IDEAS

Hetzel, J. (1993). *Responding to literature*. Cypress, CA: Creative Teaching Press.

Hoyt, L. (1999). *Revisit, reflect, retell*. Portsmouth, NH: Heinemann.

Moen, C.B. (1992). *Better than book reports*. New York: Scholastic Professional.